unravelling Psalm 91

Alex Ndukwe

Copyright © 2020 Alex Ndukwe

All rights reserved

This book or any portion thereof may not be reproduced or used without the express written permission of the publisher except for the use of brief quotations in a book review

First printing, 2020

Printed in the united states of America

ISBN: 978-1-79484-320-2

DEDICATION

I Dedicate this book to **REV Sam Bode-Lawal**, Senior Pastor at Hope Alive Christian Centre. An Erudite Bible Scholar and a Compassionate Man of God.

Forward

We need to understand some certain principles and its application to any scripture that is already existing, you will hear some men of God make assertions that Psalm 91 is very powerful. Without mincing words, we need to recall that there is power in the tongue and this transcends to the confessions we make.

Decrees and declarations can reshape our destinies and put it on a fast lane , we should be weary of God's principles this is the factor that determines if we can maintain a cordial relationship with God and holiness is very key, Hebrew 12:14 , 'Follow peace with all men, and holiness, without which no man shall see the Lord:'

It is pertinent to note that psalm 91 give us a snapshot of how the almighty can take care of our issues with involvement of Angels. It is a great privilege for every child of God to enjoy this coverage, we must understand that it can only be extended to a certified child of God.

We must strive to maintain our position, pretenders cannot enjoy the promises this psalm provides.

Table of contents

	Page
Introduction	7 - 10

Chapter 1
Secret place of the most high   11 - 17

Chapter 2
Refuge and fortress   18 - 27

Chapter 3
Deliverance from evil   28 - 78

Chapter 4
Debunk all fears   79 - 96

Chapter 5
Dominion Unleashed   97 - 107

Chapter 6

Longevity Assured 108 - 113

Introduction

Psalm 91 was written by Moses when the children of Israel were in the wilderness, the scripture was aimed at comforting the church during the 40 years curse.

This chapter is conceived as very powerful today, most Christians recite it on daily basis, this book, however, attempts at unravelling the mysteries behind it and my prayer is that the holy spirit will help us in the explanation in the name of Jesus.

It remains a powerful psalm in the bible, most children of God memorize, always recite and it is adjudged to be very powerful, there have been a series of testimonies shared concerning its efficacy. This psalm was composed by Moses while ascending into the cloud hovering over mount Sinai(Exodus 24:18), at which time he

Unravelling Psalm 91

recited these words as protection from the angels of destruction.

He that dwelleth in the secret place of the most High shall abide under the shadow of the Almighty. I will say of the LORD, He is my refuge and my fortress: my God; in him will I trust. Surely, he shall deliver thee from the snare of the fowler, and from the noisome pestilence. He shall cover thee with his feathers, and under his wings shalt thou trust: his truth shall be thy shield and buckler. Thou shalt not be afraid for the terror by night; nor for the arrow that flieth by day; Nor for the pestilence that walketh in darkness; nor for the destruction that wasteth at noonday. A thousand shall fall at thy side, and ten thousand at thy right hand; but it shall not come nigh thee. Only with thine eyes shalt thou behold and see the reward of the wicked. Because thou hast made the LORD, which is my refuge, even the most High, thy habitation; There shall no evil befall thee, neither shall any plague come nigh thy dwelling. For he shall give his angels charge over thee, to keep

thee in all thy ways. They shall bear thee up in their hands, lest thou dash thy foot against a stone. Thou shalt tread upon the lion and adder: the young lion and the dragon shalt thou trample under feet. Because he hath set his love upon me, therefore will I deliver him: I will set him on high, because he hath known my name. He shall call upon me, and I will answer him: I will be with him in trouble; I will deliver him, and honour him. With long life will I satisfy him, and show him my salvation.

This psalm dispels every danger and every contrary plan of the enemy, we ought to recite it with enormous faith and ensure its beyond just any literature rather let us expect that no evil shall befall us and will come to pass in the name of Jesus.

The secret place of the most high is likened to the inner sanctuary of the tabernacle referred to as 'holies of holies', God dwells in this place, the ark of the covenant is kept there. Can you imagine when you dwell in such a place, though at this period it might not be possible because it is not a part of the sanctuary opened or available to everyone?

This psalm invokes the power of God concerning any circumstances and at the end of the day victory songs remain on our lips, I have heard testimonies of someone that was saved in a ghastly motor accident and we could see the power of God evident, the vehicle did not look as if anyone could come out of it alive.

We have neglected the effective use of our bible and it's time for us to go back to it and ensure that the power in the word works for us in the name of Jesus, other psalms are very powerful but our focus in this book is psalm 91 and the Lord will grant us divine protection.

Chapter 1

The secret place of the most high

According to the psalmist, he who dwelt in the secret place of the most high shall abide under the shadow of the almighty. First and foremost, who is qualified to dwell in the secret place of the Almighty? Not everyone will have the privilege to dwell there and this is where the issue of relationship with God comes into play. Holiness(Hebrew 12:14), purity of hearts(Mathew 5: 8) and no wonder the psalmist in plasm 51 says 'Create in me a clean heart, O God; and renew a right spirit within me' in verse 10, the reason is not farfetched because without a clean heart there is a disconnection with the ancient of days and in verse 11, 'Cast me not away from thy presence; and take not thy holy spirit from me.' Then how can you find your way to this secret place?

Reciting this psalm is not the ultimate but fulfilling the prerequisite mentioned in the first paragraph is mandatory for every child of God, one challenge in Christendom is the pretence and we are not ready to adhere to the principles laid down by God, Apostle Peter in the book of Acts 10:34-35 says, 'Then Peter opened his mouth, and said, Of a truth, I perceive that God is no respecter of persons: But in every nation he that feareth him, and worketh righteousness, is accepted with him' and I have a question for you now, are you accepted by God, can God vouch for you?

Holy of holies might not be the correct description of the secret place of the most high, then what is this secret place. A "secret" place can also mean a difficult place to find. It is something that is not known to most people. The place is so hidden that it takes a lot of effort, energy, and sacrifice for a person to find it.

The secret place isn't reserved for lazy, wicked, and apathetic people. It isn't for the people who don't see the value of being with their Creator. After all, would God allow someone to be part of His dwelling place if that person doesn't even respect its Owner? Thus, the righteous should exert every effort to find the place of refuge. While searching for this secret place can be difficult, you and I can be assured that once we found it, we can look back and tell ourselves, "It was all worth it."

God does not test us because He wants us to suffer or prevent us from obtaining eternal life, but He does that to help us develop the godly character needed to stay with Him through thick and thin. In short: the secret place is reserved for those people who love God and do His commandments. This secret place is guarded by the most powerful, supreme, and almighty Being. No one can breach its defences. No one!

There's no doubt; God's secret place is the safest in the universe! Can you now see how God protects His people and how His people can live their lives with the incredible confidence in the fact that God shields them from harm? Indeed, if you want someone to protect you, then let it be God.

Take a deep Reflection and ask yourself the following questions:

Are you striving to dwell in God's secret place?

Are you constantly looking for ways to stay close to God?

Do you have that yearning to be on God's side every single moment of your life?

I hope your answer to these questions is yes and if not, then let us change the way we live. God is eager and is more than willing to take care of you. All you must do is stay in God's secret place and be at peace with Him.

Once we can gain access to this secret place, we will abide under the 'shadow of the almighty', the shadow of the Almighty brings to mind how a mother bird would cast her wings over her young to provide shade and protection. Abiding under the shadow of God means choosing to make it our home. We are not just to be temporary dwellers, who just come and go. We must not be strangers who would stay for a few hours, could be likened to the pillar of cloud God used to shelter the sojourning Israelites from the blazing heat of the sun as they travel across the hot wilderness. Let us look at what the 'shadow of the almighty' can do for us:

protects you from harm. All kinds of danger will not in any away affect us when we dwell under his shadow. Forces of darkness are repelled, no matter the antics the enemy wants to adopt, full protection is assured.

God's shadow brings life. The shadow of God is diametrically OPPOSITE to the shadow of death mentioned in Psalms 23. In God's shadow, it brings life. It does not bring destruction, but rather it preserves the life and health of His people.

God's shadow provides comfort. We all know how comforting it is to be under a shade. When we work outside our home, we don't want to stay too long under the sun. When we play outside, we appreciate it when the sun is not as hot as it is during noonday. We are more comfortable under the shade rather than be in the middle of a dessert.

God's shadow brings inner peace. When you look at any shadow, you know that its source is just near it. In the same way that when we choose to live under God's shadow, we have the confidence that God is just near you.

God's shadow gives joy. When you start to enjoy the benefits of abiding under God's care, it is just a matter of time when you will be filled with not just happiness, but also joyfulness and blessedness. When you see how God brings protection, life, comfort, and peace, you can't help it but be joyful, knowing that you are living the best life ever!

God's Shadow provides confidence. It's an insurance cover provided by God and we feel save knowing fully well that we are under the cover of the creator of heaven and earth, all-powerful God with an outstretched arm, nothing can be difficult for God to handle, no iota of evil can come near our dwelling.

Chapter 2

Refuge and fortress

This is a recap and a reminder of the attributes of the almighty, some see it as the other names of God. What is the meaning of these words? The refuge is defined as the state of being safe or sheltered from pursuit, danger, or difficulty and fortress, a military stronghold, especially a strongly fortified town.

Then when God is regarded as the refuge this implies that safety is guaranteed as a result of shelter provided in the secret place, we discussed in the first chapter, danger or difficulty is averted as a result of being in his abode. This is the greatest protection man can enjoy, physically man tries to provide heavy security architecture interestingly these gadgets are not responsible for our safety. Have you imagined the security man sleeps while on duty because it is God that protects his own?

The fortress is the strong security network installed by the Lord in his abode, legions of Angels are on guard and no interference from any quarters can affect us and this would give us confidence and peace of mind.   Whom can we take refuge in?, psalm 18:2 indicates that it's the Lord Almighty the creator of heaven and earth, ''The LORD is my rock, my fortress, and my deliverer. My God is my rock, in whom I take refuge, my shield, and the horn of my salvation, my stronghold. The same scripture describes the Lord as 'rock', 'deliverer', 'shield', 'horn of my salvation' and 'stronghold'. We will look at the meaning of these words and phrase before we continue with our discussion. Rock – A symbol of God in the Old Testament (1 Samuel 2:2 ; 2 Sam 22:3 ; Isaiah 17:10 ; Psalms 28:1 ; Psalms 31:2 Psalms 31:3 ; 89:26 ; 95:1); also in the New Testament (Matthew 16:18 ; Romans 9:33 ; 1 Corinthians 10:4). In Daniel 2:45 the Chaldaic form of the Hebrew word is translated "mountain." It ought to be translated "rock," as in Habakkuk 1:12 in the Revised Version. The "rock" from which the stone is cut there signifies the divine origin of Christ. (See STONE .)

The rock is a symbol of hardness (Jeremiah 5:3; compare Isaiah 50:7). Therefore, the breaking of the rock exemplifies the power of God (Jeremiah 23:29; compare 1 Kings 19:11). The rock is also a symbol of that which endures, "Oh that they .... were graven in the rock forever!" (Job 19:23,24). Rock was an appropriate place for offering a sacrifice (Judges 6:20; 13:19). The central feature of the Mosque of `Umar in Jerusalem is Qubbat-uc-Cakhrat, the "dome of the rock." The rock or cakhrat under the dome is thought to be the site of Solomon's altar of burnt offering, and further is thought to be the site of the threshing-floor of Araunah the Jebusite which David purchased to build an altar to Yahweh.

Deliverer - God delivers as he does is a polemic against the pagan rulers who challenge his ability to rescue his people. Nebuchadnezzar (Daniel 3:15 Daniel 3:28), Pharaoh (Exod 5:2), and Sennacherib (2 Chron 32:10-15) railed against Israel for trusting in God's deliverance. The subsequent rescue serves as a demonstration of

God's ability to deliver his people from the most powerful worldly forces.

While God is the great deliverer, there are no manipulative ploys by his people to effect his intervention. All Acts of deliverance are his initiative and express his mercy and his love (Psalm 51:1; 71:2; 86:13). Therefore, there is no one to rescue the ungodly (Psalm 50:22). God's deliverance is for his people, those who trust and fear him: "To the faithful, you show yourself faithful You save the humble but bring low those whose eyes are haughty" (Psalms 18:25 Psalms 18:27). Often, the people's fear of God and trust in him are seen as a part of the deliverance (Psalm 22:4; 33:18-19; 34:7; Ezek 14:20). Their righteousness preserves them (Prov 11:6; Ezekiel 14:14 Ezekiel 14:20) but if they indulge in sin and rebellion, God may deliver them over to their enemies (1 Kings 8:46; Jer 20:5; Ezek 11:8-9).

Shield - used in defensive warfare, varying at different times and under different circumstances in size, form, and material (1 Samuel 17:7; 2 Sam 1:21; 1 Kings 10:17; 1 Chronicles 12:8 1 Chronicles 12:24 1 Chronicles 12:34; Isaiah 22:6; Ezekiel 39:9; Nahum 2:3). Used figuratively of God and earthly princes as the defenders of their people (Genesis 15:1; Deuteronomy 33:29; Psalms 33:20; 84:11). Shields were usually "anointed" (Isaiah 21:5), to preserve them, and at the same time make the missiles of the enemy glide off them more easily.

horn of my salvation

The horn of salvation is mentioned several times in the Bible, but what does this expression mean? What does salvation have to do with a horn?

In the Old Testament, the word horn signifies many things. Of course, one usage of a horn was to refer to a pointed bony structure growing out of an animal's head (Genesis 22:13). Animal horns, used for fighting, protection, and securing dominance, became symbols of strength, power, and victory.

Often, Scripture's mention of a "horn" is as a literary symbol representing potency and power.

For example, in Daniel 7:7 and 24, the ten horns of Daniel's fourth beast represent ten kings. In Psalm 75:10, God says, "I will cut off the horns of all the wicked, but the horns of the righteous will be lifted." In other words, the righteous will prevail, no matter how strong the wicked seem to be. In Jeremiah 48:25, "Moab's horn is cut off" means that the strength of Moab is gone. The four horns in Zechariah 1:18–19 represent the powerful nations that attacked and scattered Israel.

Animal horns were also used as receptacles for oil (1 Samuel 16:1) or as a shofar trumpet (Joshua 6:5). The prayer in Psalm 92:10 contains both a reference to oil and figurative use of horn: "You have exalted my horn like that of a wild ox; fine oils have been poured on me."

In 1 Samuel 2:1 Hannah prays, "In the Lord, my horn is lifted high," indicating the strength that will come from her having a child. In Luke 1:69 Zechariah praises God that "He has raised a horn of salvation for us in the house of his servant David." In this case, the "horn of salvation" is a reference to Jesus Christ, the powerful deliverer and king who was soon to be born.

Another significant instance of the word horn in the Old Testament is about the protrusion at each corner of the altar (Exodus 27:2). In worship, the horns of the altar were dabbed with blood to purify them and make atonement for sin (Leviticus 8:15; 4:6). The horns of the altar speak of the power of God's salvation. That part of the altar also became a place of refuge and sanctuary for a fugitive (1 Kings 1:50).

We often see the horn in Scripture as a symbol of salvation. Psalm 18:2 says, "The LORD is my rock and my fortress and my deliverer, my God, my rock, in whom I take refuge, my shield, and the horn of my salvation, my stronghold." In the New Testament, Jesus is the horn of salvation (Luke 1:68–69). Thus, a title applied to Yahweh is also applied to Jesus; they are both called "the horn of salvation." The very name Jesus means "The Lord Is Salvation." The salvation Jesus offers is strong, triumphant, and powerful. Just like the horns on the altar offered refuge and atonement, Jesus offers clemency and cleansing through His death on the cross. However strong our spiritual foe, the horn of our salvation is stronger still.

Stronghold

A stronghold is defined as "1. a place that has been fortified to protect it against attack; 2. a place where a particular cause or belief is strongly defended or upheld." Strongholds are designed to be a safe place. As believers in Christ, we need to make the Lord our stronghold. He is our safe place and refuge (Psalm 27:1).

The Lord has remained our refuge, fortress which portrays the fact that God is our rock, Deliverer, horn of our salvation, stronghold and as his children, we must not forget this in a hurry no matter what we are presently passing through or experiencing, the psalmist says in psalm 62:11,

'God has spoken once; I have heard this twice: that power belongs to God.' I want to remind us that the Lord is powerful and you could imagine as we explained the phrase, 'horn of my salvation', the animal uses the horn to protect itself by fighting, this indicates that one hundred per cent protection is guaranteed but we must recall that there is the prerequisite that we must fulfil and it's out of place to memorize Psalm 91 without living a holy life and trusting the Lord.

Trusting the Lord should be as a result of his track record, Israelites were delivered from the bondage that had lasted for 430 years, I am not worried about the assertion of the bible scholars that will say after all these must happen so that the prophecies would be fulfilled, the Lord was indeed the Refuge and fortress of the children of Israel.

The enemy is aware that God is the Refuge and fortress of his children and that was the reason why Satan negotiated with him so that Job will be tempted and wanted to prove that Job will forsake him and I believe we know the remaining story of the travails of the man called Job.

Jesus Christ has the same attribute as God the father, in this case, the name performs this task for us, my bible tells me in Philippians 2: 10-11,' that at the name of Jesus every knee should bow, in heaven and on earth and under the earth, and every tongue confess that Jesus Christ is Lord, to the glory of God the Father....' this is the reason why most people around the globe shout 'JESUS' when in danger or under severe threat.

Chapter 3

Deliverance from evil

Though we have mentioned deliverance in chapter two, with this chapter we will dwell more on this topic and ensure justice is done to it. Satan is the source of evil to man and we should appreciate that we wrestle not against flesh and blood but principalities, power and rulers of the darkness of this world. (Ephesians 6:12). The battles we are confronted with are not physical and we must depend on the almighty to help us in this challenge.

Can you recall the experience of DANIEL, this story is recorded in Daniel 10:13, 'However, the prince of the kingdom of Persia opposed me for twenty-one days. Then Michael, one of the chief princes, came to help me, for I had been left there with the kings of Persia.'

This angel was trapped for twenty-one days at the Kingdom of Persia, a contrary power that is considered principalities and there was nothing he could do to rescue himself, the Lord discovered this challenge and sent Angel Michael and archangel regarded as chief princes to proceed to that Kingdom and rescue this angel.

If an angel could pass through this and we must understand that it is only God that can deliver, and this could come in different dimensions, but the bottom line remains that powers must change hands and victory comes alive.

The truth of the matter is that we must exercise faith in a midst of a storm and we must look beyond the limitations currently experienced, this accounts for the reason why God had to send his only begotten son to this world, apart from saving us from our sins, his coming was to also to retrieve the keys of heaven and hell. Prophecies that were recorded years before his birth, Isaiah 9:6, 'For unto us a child is born, unto us, a son is given: and the government shall be upon his shoulder: and his name shall be called Wonderful,

Counsellor, The mighty God, The everlasting Father, The Prince of Peace.'

Politics and government. We seem to see them as necessary evils, bringing frustration in the present but still giving us hope for the future. Our contradictory attitudes about politics are revealing. We recognize the failure of human solutions, but at the same time, we know something must be done to fix what's broken in the world. What man can't do; God has done; He's given the Messiah.

Isaiah wrote this prophecy at least a hundred years before Israel was taken into Babylonian captivity—nearly 600 years before the birth of the Savior! Looking at a litany of failed monarchs, and sitting in the rubble of Israel's monarchy, Isaiah looked across the centuries to a time when God would rule on earth through His Son. "A child will be born to us" underscores the Messiah's humanity. He had to come as a human being, in the form of a child, so He could endure the temptations men face, yet be without sin (Hebrews 4:15).

"A son will be given to us" implies the Savior's deity. He existed before His birth as the second Person of the Trinity: "Although He existed in the form of God, did not regard equality with God a thing to be grasped, but emptied Himself, taking the form of a bond-servant, and being made in the likeness of men" (Philippians 2:6-7). He came as the Son of God—God in human flesh—to conquer sin and death forever.

"The government will rest on His shoulders" affirms His lordship. This verse looks to a time still future when Christ will reign over a literal, earthly, geopolitical kingdom that encompasses all the kingdoms and governments of the world (cf. Daniel 2:44; Zechariah 14:9).

In that day, the government of the whole world will rest on His shoulders. But until that time, His kingdom is in an invisible form (cf. Luke 17:20-21). The Messiah's rule is over those who trust Him and obey Him as Lord. It's currently an invisible kingdom, but will one day become visible and universal as His rule extends even over those who do not acknowledge His lordship in their hearts.

What kind of kingdom is it? What distinguishes the Messiah's kingdom from the other kingdoms of this world? The names Israel used for Christ in a hint at four characteristics that make the Messiah's kingdom—in all its manifestations—different from any other earthly government. At a time when the world is weary and despairing of political solutions when the political future looks bleak, this is welcome news.

First, this kingdom is free from confusion, because Christ is a "Wonderful Counsellor." The King James Version separates "Wonderful" and "Counsellor" with a comma, but the words seem to go better together and appear that way in most modern versions. Now and then, a politician comes on the scene who possesses, according to some, messiah-like qualities. Whether it's a reference to speaking ability, charisma, or wisdom, it's certainly a compliment. However, when you compare the greatest social or political leader with Jesus Christ, you'll find there's no comparison at all.

During His incarnation, Christ demonstrated His wisdom as a counsellor. While I was writing The Gospel According to Jesus, I studied every major encounter Jesus had with individuals who came to Him for counsel. He always knew what to say, when to reach out to a seeking heart, and when to rebuke an impetuous soul. Even his enemies testified, "Never did a man speak the way this man speaks" (John 7:46).

As God incarnate, Christ is the source of all truth. Jesus said, "I am the way, and the truth, and the life" (John 14:6). No politician can match that! It is He to whom we must ultimately turn and trust His loving rule of our lives. Many of our politicians turn everywhere else for counsel. They go to one another; they listen to special interests; they have their psychologists, psychiatrists, analysts, philosophers, spiritual advisors, gurus, astrologers, and other human counsellors. But the King of kings keeps His own counsel. After all, "Who has directed the Spirit of the Lord, or as His counsellor has informed Him?" (Isaiah 40:13).

The Messiah is the Wonderful Counselor because He is God, the source of truth. When He rules the earth, there will be no uncertainty in his administration. He is the ultimate and only true answer to political confusion.

Second, the Messiah's kingdom is singularly free from chaos because He is the Mighty God. He is the One who in creation brought order out of chaos. Scripture says, "God is not a God of confusion but peace" (1 Corinthians 14:33). Chaos is antithetical to who He is. He is a God of order. Christ the King is orderly, and He brings order to the troubled lives of all who surrender to Him. In other words, He not only tells His subjects what to do as a Wonderful Counselor but since He is the Mighty God, He can also energize them to do it.

Legislation can go only so far; it stops short of providing the power and the will to obey. Because of the sinful nature, people will always strain against law and order (Romans 7:8). Add human fallibility to the inability to make people obey from the heart, and you can see the severe limitations of political and legislative solutions.

But when Jesus Christ comes to rule this earth, He'll display His divine power by bringing order to the chaos. Those who do not submit to His leadership from the heart, He'll subjugate with a rod of iron (cf. Psalm 2:9; Revelation 2:27; 12:5; 19:15). Those who humble themselves from the heart, bowing to Him as Lord and Saviour, will find the power of the Mighty God unleashed in their lives to help them obey.

Because Christ is God, He can forgive sin, defeat Satan, liberate people from the power of evil, redeem them, answer their prayers, restore their broken souls, and reign as Lord—"Mighty God"—over their newly ordered lives. That's a politician this world has never seen. In comparison to human governments, the Messiah's kingdom is uncomplicated because He is the "Eternal Father." The phrase means, "Father of Eternity."

That is a clear reference to the biblical truth that Christ is Creator of heaven and earth. In Hebrews 1:10-12 God the Father says to Christ the Son, "You, Lord, in the beginning, laid the foundation of the earth, and the heavens are the works of Your hands; they will perish, but You remain, and they all will become old like a garment, and like a mantle, You will roll them up; like a garment they will also be changed. But You are the same, and Your years will not come to an end."

Nothing is too complex for the Creator and Sustainer of everything. Infinity and all its intricacies are nothing to Him who is the Alpha and Omega, the First and the Last, the Beginning and the End. Human life is getting more and more complex. Technology has so improved communication and transportation that commerce, culture, and religion have become global. And rather than organizing and making sense of it all, governments of the world seem to exist primarily to make things more complicated. We build bureaucracies to deal with the complexities of life—and consequently, life only grows more perplexing.

Messiah's government, however, is simple and uncomplicated. He is the sole ruler—no bloated bureaucracy—and He knows the end from the beginning because He is the Father of Eternity. Isaiah, prophesying about the kingdom, wrote of the highway of holiness: "The unclean shall not pass over it; but it shall be for those: the wayfaring men, though fools, shall not err therein" (Isaiah 35:8, KJV). His way is so free from the complexities of life that even fools cannot lose their way.

That kind of simplicity characterizes the Messiah's entire government. As the Father of Eternity, He alone comprehends the complexities of time and eternity. He requires no bureaucracy; He shoulders His government by Himself.

Finally, in the Messiah's kingdom, there are no conflicts because He is the Prince of Peace. He offers peace from God (Romans 1:7) to all who are the recipients of His grace. He brings peace with God (Romans 5:1) to those who surrender to Him in faith. He brings the peace of God (Philippians 4:7) to those who walk with Him.

There never really has been peace on earth in the sense we think of it. Wars and rumours of wars have characterized the entire two millennia since the announcement at His birth of peace on earth (Luke 2:14). That angelic announcement of peace on earth was a two-pronged proclamation. First, it proclaimed that God's peace is available to men and women right now. Read the words of Luke 2:14 carefully: "Glory to God in the highest, and on earth peace among men with whom He is pleased" (emphasis added).

Who are those with whom He is pleased? They are those who have yielded their lives to the authority of His government: "The Lord taketh pleasure in them that fear him, in those that hope in his mercy" (Psalm 147:11, KJV). Why should we hope in His mercy? Because we are sinners who need His forgiveness (Romans 3:23). We must recognize that fact first of all if we are to place our lives under His government. We must understand that He gave His own sinless, guiltless life on our behalf. He died for our sins to save us from God's righteous wrath (Romans 5:6-9). And we must be willing to turn from our sins and embrace Him by faith, realizing that we can never earn His favour (Ephesians 2:8-9).

But secondly, the angel's announcement of "peace on earth" declared the arrival of the only One who ultimately can bring lasting peace on earth. Jesus Christ will bring lasting peace in the final establishment of His earthly kingdom. As we already mentioned, He will ensure "peace on earth" over the rebellious at heart by wielding a "rod of iron." There will be no coup d'état, no insurrection, not even the slightest threat to disturb the peace He brings to the world.

Isaiah 9:7 continues, "There will be no end to the increase of His government or peace." In other words, His government and peace will keep expanding and improving. The familiar hymn "Like a River Glorious" accurately speaks of the peace that is "perfect, yet it floweth fuller every day, Perfect, yet it groweth deeper all the way." How can anything perfect improve? That's one of the mysteries of Messiah's government. It gets better and better, and perfect peace flows deeper and deeper. I look forward to the day when He returns to execute the final political solution that will truly bring world peace. His is the greatest government because it's ruled by the greatest ruler—the "Wonderful Counsellor, Mighty God, Eternal Father, Prince of Peace." He is the only hope of mankind.

I also hope the government of your life is on His shoulders, that He rules and reigns even now in your heart. Only then will you experience the growing peace that comes only from the Prince of Peace.

We have seen that 'JESUS' remains the battle Axe and weapon of war(Jerimiah 50:20) that God the father has released to mankind and without mincing words, in Christendom today we are not ready to crack bones but to continue to breastfeed on milk and it's pertinent to note that adults with grey beards are still breastfeeding and have refused to learn to crack bones. We must take our rightful positions in our society and our presence must be felt.

Let us continue with our discussion, can I ask you a simple question, 'Who are you?', the answers would come in diverse directions but we must not forget that we are 'Children of God' and Romans 8:17 clearly states that, 'And if children, then heirs; heirs of God, and joint-heirs with Christ; if so be that we suffer with him, that we may be also glorified together.'

I want to appreciate God for this wonderful privilege handed to us and we must ensure we take advantage of this, we need to understand that we lay claim of the inheritance and that is the beauty of being the heir of God and Joint-heir with Christ. We need not forget that they are a different kind of children of God and you should understand where I'm heading to, in your heart now take a critical look at yourself, its either you are on track with Jesus or you are out of the track, this decides if you can claim the inheritance as we have indicated. The issue of identity must be resolved in our hearts and this is very vital.

Isaiah 22:22 shed more light on the attribute of the messiah that is to come, 'The key of the house of David I will lay on his shoulder; So he shall open, and no one shall shut, And he shall shut, and no one shall open.' Jerimiah 51:20-23 also says 'Thou art my battle axe and weapons of war: for with thee will I break in pieces the nations, and with thee will I destroy kingdoms; And with thee will I break in pieces the horse and his rider; and with thee will I break in pieces the chariot and his rider; With thee also will I break in pieces man and woman; and with thee will I break in pieces old and young; and with thee will I break in pieces the young man and the maid; I will also break in pieces with thee the shepherd and his flock; and with thee will I break in pieces the husbandman and his yoke of oxen; and with thee will I break in pieces captains and rulers.'

The key of the house of David I will lay on his shoulder, these keys of David upon the shoulder of Jesus is dominion over principalities, Power and anything that seems unpleasant, even powers that are yet to be invented. Been the heir according to Romans 8:17, we also continue to possess the key of David upon our shoulder too and when we make decrees and declarations it shall be established and such spoken words will not in any way fall to the ground, as it is spoken heaven puts seal upon it which typifies approval, nobody can stop it even powers from the pit of hell cannot stop it from coming to pass and that's the reason the scripture says '……So he shall open, and no one shall shut; And he shall shut, and no one shall open.', this power has been handed to you via inheritance and you technically become the battle-axe and weapon of war, there is no war you cannot fight and the Lord would make you victorious.

The accounts of the Lamb of God during his earthly ministry was to help us strengthen our faith and also ensure we do greater works than the master did and I want to appreciate God for the prophecies that came to pass concerning Jesus, during his crucifixion the world felt that they have destroyed this so-called king of the Jews but not knowing that power of resurrection was released for future use, Acts of apostle provides evidence that the power was still in existence, with diverse miracles and John 14:12 came into fulfilment.

Divine Protection

'He shall cover thee with his feathers, and under his wings shalt thou trust: his truth shall be thy shield and buckler.'

Consider what happens when an eagle attempts to carry a chicken, mother hen protects them by covering them under her wings, this illustration is similar to how the almighty protects his own and we must understand that God's protection over us can be beyond our understanding.

This is intriguing considering the population of children of God scattered all over the world and you can imagine that God is still able to place them under his wings and this shows that the Almighty is exceedingly great for providing such coverage.

Placing his children 'under his wings' is indeed spiritual and when this verse 4 of Psalm 91 is recited automatically you invoke the power of God and protection can come in diverse ways and they are as follows:

- hedge of Protection
- Wall of Fire around his children coverage with the garment of Light
- Long Outstretched Arm

- shield of Faith
- Angels on Assignment
- Spiritual Armour of God is released upon his Children

Hedge of protection

What is the hedge of protection? , In the first chapter of Job, God points out to Satan that Job is "blameless and upright, a man who fears God and shuns evil" (Job 1:8). Satan replies, "Does Job fear God for nothing?...Have you not put a hedge around him and his household and everything he has?" (verses 9–10). Though most children of God pray for a hedge of protection, the beauty of the story here is that verse 4 of Psalm 91 invokes the 'hedge of protection' and this forms the basis of God placing his children under his wings. I don't want to be misquoted you are free to pray for the hedge of protection.

In the time of the Old Testament, wild animals were much more prevalent in the Middle East than they are today. The Bible mentions lions (Judges 14:5), wolves (Jeremiah 5:6), bears (1 Samuel 17:34), leopards (Hosea 13:7), and hyenas (Isaiah 13:22).

Although stone walls could keep predators away from living areas and livestock, the walls would have to be very tall and would take a long time to make. Wood was not plentiful enough to waste on a fence. Instead, a hedge of thorn bushes could be induced to grow around a living compound.

Thorn bushes would be too dense to crawl through, too sharp to chew through, and too deep for all but the most determined leopard to jump over. A hedge would also be a deterrent to sheep and goats seeking to escape their pen. As Satan is compared to a "lion looking for someone to devour" (1 Peter 5:8), a thorn hedge is an appropriate metaphor for the protection God gives His followers.

Unravelling Psalm 91

Wall of Fire around his children

Zechariah 2:5, 'For I will be a wall of fire around it, declares the LORD, and I will be the glory within it.', though bible scholars might argue that this scripture is speaking concerning Jerusalem and I want to remind you that God's children are also his building, 1 Corinthians 3:9, '"For we are God's fellow workers; you are God's field, you are God's building.", this scripture applies and we need to understand that God can be a wall of fire around his children is another type of protection. God's Glory is also within and this shows that when we have the fire surrounding us, his glory is also within and this serves as a seal that could be detected in the spiritual realm, even the enemies will also discover this and they keep away from children of God.

coverage with the garment of Light

God, Himself is encircled by what Scripture calls a garment of light. Psalm 104:1-2 says, "O Lord my God...You are clothed with honour and majesty—

Unravelling Psalm 91

[You are the One] Who covers Yourself with light as with a garment..." (The Amplified Bible).

Adam was created in God's image and God "crowned him with glory and honour" (Psalm 8:5). A Jewish commentary on Psalm 93 tells us, "As he sang God's praises, Adam truly looked Divine, because he was a reflection of God's image." Think about it—Adam looked just like God. He was clothed in the glory of God—he wore a garment of light.

Now it's true when Adam sinned, the glory departed from him. He lost that crown of honour. But thank God, Jesus got back everything in the redemption that Adam lost in the Fall. As believers in Christ, we are temples of the living God. He goes everywhere we go when we are filled with Him. God lives in us and we should radiate His presence and love.

He has covered us with a garment, or shield, of light. We may not always be able to see it, but rest assured, beings in the spirit realm (including devils and demons) see and recognize the glory of God on us. Occasionally, this light is visible in the natural too. The garment of

Long Outstretched Arm

Jerimiah 32:17-18, 'Ah Lord GOD! behold, thou hast made the heaven and the earth by thy great power and stretched out arm, and there is nothing too hard for thee: Outstretched arm of the Lord could equally protect his children from any form of danger, this implies that God could trigger some events to occur and this would lead to our protection. During danger, with the power of God supernatural events occur and leads to our protection and deliverance. Paul and Silas were thrown into Maximum security prison, Acts 16:25 indicated that they prayed and sang praises and there was an earthquake and the prison doors opened and their bonds were loosed.

God with an outstretched arm will cause the supernatural to happen which guarantees our protection, in case of the Children of Israel on their way out of Egypt, Pillar of Cloud arose, and this was a demonstration of God's power and the children of Israel were protected.

shield of Faith

The shield of faith is part of the Armor of God described in Ephesians 6:10–17. After summarizing the gospel and giving the Ephesians various instructions, Paul concludes his missive to them saying, in part, "Finally, be strong in the Lord and his mighty power. Put on the Full Armor of God, so that you can take your stand against the devil's schemes" (Ephesians 6:10–11). About the shield, Paul writes, "In addition to all this, take up the shield of faith, with which you can extinguish all the flaming arrows of the evil one" (verse 16). The ESV puts it this way: "In all circumstances take up the shield of faith, with which you can extinguish all the flaming darts of the evil one."

The Roman shield of the time was called a scutum. This type of shield was as large as a door and would cover the warrior entirely. Such a shield was not just defensive but could also be used to push opponents. When fighting as a group, a phalanx of soldiers could position their shields to form an enclosure around themselves, called a testudo ("tortoise"). This was especially helpful to protect against arrows launched from the walls of cities they were attacking. Shields, often made of wood and then covered in hiding, when wet, could extinguish flaming arrows.

A shield is vitally important to a soldier. It provides a blanket of protection. It is meant to be taken up in all circumstances. It is the first barrier against the enemy's attack. Often, shields were painted with identifying marks; a Christian who takes up the shield of faith identifies himself as a foot soldier who serves the Commander of the Lord's army (see Joshua 5:14).

Hebrews 11:1 says, "Now faith is confidence in what we hope for and assurance about what we do not see." Verse 6 stresses the importance of faith: "Without faith, it is impossible to please God." Satan's attacks can sometimes cause us to doubt God. Faith prompts us to believe in God. We give in to temptation when we believe what it has to offer is better than what God has promised. Faith reminds us that, though the fulfilment of God's promise may not be readily visible to us, God is true to His Word. When Satan attempts to plague us with doubt or entice us with instant gratification, faith recognizes the deceptiveness of his tactics and quickly extinguishes the arrows. When Satan accuses us, faith chooses to believe that Jesus has redeemed us and that there is no more condemnation (Romans 8:1, 34; Revelation 12:10–12).

Faith is one of the greatest gifts (1 Corinthians 13:13), and it is how we receive grace and come into right relationship with God (Ephesians 2:8–9). It is because we have been justified through faith that we belong to God and have peace with Him (Romans 5:1). Faith is the doorway to hope in God (Romans 5:2). Because we have faith in God, our suffering need not faze us; in fact, we can persevere under it (Romans 5:3–5). The things Satan attempts to use to discourage us can become tools in the hands of God.

All believers have this promise: "Everyone born of God overcomes the world. This is the victory that has overcome the world, even our faith" (1 John 5:4). Faith is a protective barrier between us and the schemes of Satan. When we believe God and take Him at His word, we remain grounded in truth, the lies of the enemy lose their power, and we become overcomers. In that way, faith is our shield.

Angels on Assignment

'he shall give his angels charge over thee, to keep thee in all thy ways. They shall bear thee up in their hands, lest thou dash thy foot against a stone.'

We are living in the times where the ministry of angels is being restored to the Church. Because we are in a season of heightened angelic activity, now is the time to learn to work with the angels of heaven to fulfil your destiny on earth. The angels of heaven that are assigned to you are now welcoming you to their realm that will take you to a higher level in God. Angels are a part of the Kingdom of heaven. As Kingdom warriors, we can expect to experience angelic activity to be an integral part of the Kingdom life of every Christian. We are now living in the last days where everything is being accelerated. Walking close with God and working with angels is a required mandate for those that desire to be part of the move of God that is now taking place on earth.

Jesus prayer is for "Thy Kingdom come; thy will be done on earth as it is in heaven" (Mt. 6:10). That which takes place in heaven is also to take place on earth. Because angels do the will of God they are enlisted to help the Church establish His Kingdom on earth as it is in heaven. In God's Kingdom, there is no illness, sickness, demonic activity or disease. Angels are on assignment to assist you! The apostle Paul understood this relationship between the Church and angels declaring, "Are they not all ministering spirits, sent forth to minister for them who shall be heirs of salvation? (He. 1:14).

The call of the Church is to plunder the gates of hell and establish the rule of Christ through the preaching of the gospel of the Kingdom. This is the commission given by Jesus who said, "And as you go, preach and say, the Kingdom of heaven is at hand, heal the sick, raise the dead, cast out devils, freely you have received freely give" (Mt. 10:7-8). The invasion of God on earth comes through a people that have received power from on high that have learned to release it into every circumstance of life. We were born to rule over darkness by preaching the gospel message of His Kingdom.

For the prayer of Jesus to be fulfilled for "Thy Kingdom Come" that is established through the gospel message of the Kingdom, we must embrace the entire realm of His Kingdom. This includes the ministry of angels. Ministering angels are sent to help assist in the work of ministry – every Church should have at least one!

to minister with our assigned angels will ramp up the anointing that reveals the Kingdom of heaven to a lost and dying world in unprecedented power. New beginnings are now upon us with great opportunities to engage with the angels of heaven that will take you to the next level of Kingdom life in your walk with Christ.

Angels have always played an important role in the history of mankind to fulfil the purpose of God. From the book of Genesis to the book of Revelation there are numerous accounts by those that have received angelic visitation. Some of these visitations came to men through a vision, a dream, or the physical appearance of an angel.

God has angels on assignment. We just need to be aware of them and learn how to properly respond to work with them. As I have studied the scriptures I have not only been greatly encouraged by their ministry but my spiritual awareness of the Kingdom of heaven is elevated to a whole new level.

Unravelling Psalm 91

The following are but a few of the Biblical accounts of angelic visitations. I have organized these accounts according to the angel's purpose. I pray that these Biblical accounts will enhance your awareness of angelic activity as well as a greater awareness of the Kingdom of heaven that is available to you from on high.

Jacob saw in a dream angels ascending and descending on a ladder that bridged the gap between heaven and earth with God standing on top of it! And he dreamed and behold a ladder set up on the earth, and the top of it reached to heaven: and behold the angels of God ascending and descending on it. And behold, the Lord stood on top of it... And Jacob was afraid, and said, "How dreadful this place is! This is none other but the house of God, and this is the gate of heaven" (Ge. 28:12, 13, 17).

Jacob called the place Bethel, which means "the house of God" because it was the gate of heaven. There are places on earth that God has established as stairways for heavenly activity, such as Moravian Falls in North Carolina. Moravian Falls is known to be very high on the scale of angelic activity. I can personally attest that this is true.

Some ministries have open heaven where the people regularly receive an outpouring of the Holy Spirit. The church is called to be an open portal to host His presence. A stairway for angels to ascend and descend as well as a place where the Lord stands over it as it's covering. Every born again believer and church are called to be a "Bethel," a stairway to heaven where angels come and go.

Angels provide direction and guidance – Moses worked with an angel that was assigned to direct his path as Israel travelled through the wilderness. The Lord told Moses not to offend him and to pay strict attention to his words! Behold, I send an angel before you, to keep you in the way, and to bring you into the place which I have prepared. Beware of him and obey his voice, provoke him not; for he will not pardon your transgressions, for My name is written in him (Exodus 23:20-21).

Notice that the Lord tells Moses, "Behold I send an angel before you to keep you in the way and to bring you into the place that I have prepared." Angels are assigned to keep you and they go before you to bring you into the place of your destiny! When I travel the Lord has often sent an angel before me to prepare the way for my arrival in safety.

The Lord also tells Moses 'Beware of him and obey his voice, provoke him not." We must honour the angels in our midst and make sure that we do not provoke them. Although we do not worship angels the Lord only, they are, after all, God's creation. For angels to work with us we must welcome them in our midst and treat them with great respect.

Unravelling Psalm 91

As the aforementioned scripture denotes, God promised Moses that if he obeyed the voice of the angel to do all that he tells him to do, the Lord will be an enemy to his enemies! What a working relationship Moses had with God and his assigned angel!

But if you shall indeed obey his voice, and do all that I speak; then I will be an enemy unto your enemies, and adversary unto your adversary. For my, Angel shall go before you before the Amorites....and I will cut them off (Exodus 23:22-23).

Another Biblical example of angels providing guidance is when an angel spoke to Philip telling him to go to the South where he would meet an Ethiopian. "And the angel of the Lord spoke to Philip, saying, Arise and go toward the South on the road that goes to Jerusalem...And he arose and went" (Acts 8:26-27). Because of this direction, Philip led the Ethiopian man to Christ. There is nothing like getting a clear direction to multiply the effectiveness of your ministry!

Angels of War– An angel appeared to Joshua as a man of war with a sword in his hand. As the captain of the Lord of Host, he came to lead the army of Israel into battle to take possession of the Promised Land. This event signified a transition for Israel with the anointing to make a shift from wandering around in the wilderness to defeating their enemies. Angels can assist you in spiritual warfare to defeat your enemies.

And it came to pass when Joshua was by Jericho, that he lifted his eyes and looked, and behold, there stood a man over against him with his sword drawn in his hand: and Joshua went unto him and asked, "Are you for us or our enemies?" And he said, "Neither, but I have come as the captain of the host of the Lord…" (Joshua 5:13-14)

that the angel of the Lord appeared to Joshua as a man. You never know how an angel may appear to you. Paul tells us to love one another and practice the ministry of hospitality for you may well be "entertaining angels unaware" (He. 13:2).

An angel of the Lord came to Gideon who commissioned him to lead an army to free Israel from the oppression of their enemies, "And the angel of the Lord appeared unto him, and said to Gideon, "The Lord is with you, for you are a mighty man of valour (Judges 6:12).

Gideon went into battle, he was known by his enemies as "The sword of Gideon" for the sword of the Lord was with him. (Judges 7:14, 17). The Lord is once again equipping an army with the sword of the Lord and he will lead it, for "The Lord will go forth like a warrior. He will arouse His zeal like a man of war. He will utter a shout, yes; He will raise a war cry. He will prevail over His enemies (Is. 42:13).

Angels as messengers – The angel Gabriel came to Mary, the mother of Jesus, with the

Unravelling Psalm 91

message that the Lord will overshadow her and she would conceive a child of the Holy Spirit. (Luke 1:26-3) After Mary's immaculate conception, an angel visited Joseph in a dream with the message to take Mary as his wife, for that which is conceived in her womb is that of the Holy Spirit (Mt. 1:18-21).

After Christ resurrection, an angel from heaven rolled back the stone from the tomb of Christ and sat on it. His countenance was like lightning and his raiment white as snow. He brings the message to Mary Magdalene and her friends that Christ has risen and behold there was an earthquake: for the angel of the Lord descended from heaven, and came and rolled back the stone from the door and sat on it. His countenance was like lightning, and his raiment white as snow. And the angel said to the women, "Fear not, for I know that you seek Jesus, which was crucified. He is not here, for he has risen…" (Mt. 28:2, 3, 5-6).

Angels strengthen those in need – After Christ completed his 40 days fast in the wilderness where he was tempted by Satan, angels came and ministered to him. (Mark 1:13) An angel also ministered to Jesus in the Mount of Olives when he was faint from praying. In this case, we see that an angel strengthened Jesus to such a degree, that it empowered Him to pray even more earnestly until He sweats drops of blood.

there appeared an angel unto him from heaven, strengthening him. And being in agony, he prayed the more earnestly, and His sweat was as it were great drops of blood falling to the ground (Luke 22:43-44).

The prophet Elijah often received strength as well as direction from an angel that put his fears to rest. For example, the King of Samaria fell through a lattice and was on his death bed when he sent messengers to inquire of the god Beelzebub for a prophetic word in regards to his fate. An angel appears to Elijah and tells him to meet the Kings' messengers to give them the fateful news that the King would not recover from his wounds and will die. (2 Kings 1:3) In response to this ill-fated news, the King sends a captain with a company of 50 men to fetch Elijah to bring him back to the King so that he can inquire of him. Elijah has forewarned of their arrival and positions himself on top of a hill.

In the presence of Elijah, the captain and his band of men are consumed by the fire that fell upon them from heaven. The King hearing this news sends another 50 men to capture Elijah and thy too perished by fire. The King in his persistence sends another 50 men to fetch Elijah. This time the captain and his 50 men bow the knee and ask Elijah for mercy. Being of a different spirit, the Lord sends an angel to dispel Elijah's fears,

the angel of the Lord said to Elijah, "Go down with him, and do not be afraid of Him." So Elijah got up and went down with him to the King (2Kings 1:15).

Angels bring encouragement – Angels often bring encouragement to those that are caught in dire situations. While on his journey to Rome during a tempest storm that threatened to destroy the ship and its crew, an angel appeared to Paul with a word of good cheer that Paul passed onto the ship's crew,

And now I exhort you to be of good cheer: for there shall be no loss or any man's life among you, but of the ship. For there stood by me this night the angel of God, whose I am and whom I serve. Saying, "Fear not, Paul, you must be brought before Caesar, and lo, God has all them that sail with you. Wherefore be of good cheer: for I believe God…" (Acts 27:22-25)

Because of the working relationship that Paul had with his angel, the lives of over 200 men were saved and Paul eventually made it to Rome. It was the angel that was assigned to Paul that kept him safe on his journey. King David tells us "For He shall give His angels charge over you to keep you in all His ways" (Psalms 91:11).

The Harvest – Jesus said that in the last days a great harvest will take place. This harvest will exceed all other outpourings of the Spirit and movements of history combined. In the parable of the harvest, (Mt. 13:24-30) Jesus illustrates that angels are sent from heaven to reap the harvest.

He that sows the good seed is the Son of man. The field is the world and the good seed are the children of the kingdom, but the tares are the children of the wicked one. The enemy that sowed them is the devil: the harvest is the end of the world: and the reapers are the angels (Mathew 13:37-39). The Lord clearly states the reapers are the angels of heaven. Jesus also asked that we pray to the Lord of the harvest to send forth labourers into the harvest, for the harvest is ripe but the labourers are few. (Luke 10:2). This suggests a working relationship between the angels that reap in the harvest and the labourers that work in the harvest – those that preach the gospel message of the Kingdom.

We are living in the times where the people of God on earth and the angels of heaven will work together to bring in the harvest. The church should now position itself to care for the influx of converts that come in to care for the Lord's own and equip them for the work of ministry. Those that come in from the first harvest are to be equipped and trained to bring in the next harvest, which will be greater. Angels of deliverance – Angels often intervene to deliver God's people from certain death. Daniel's life was spared by an angel when he was thrown into the pit with the Lions. When the King looked in on him, he found Daniel safe and sound.

Then the king arose very early in the morning and went in haste unto the den of Lions. And when he came to the den, he cried with a lamentable voice unto Daniel, "O Daniel, servant of the living God, is your God, whom you serve able to deliver you from the Lions?" Then said Daniel to the King, "O King live forever. My God has sent His angel and has shut the lion's mouths, and they have not hurt me..." (Daniel 6:19-22).

During the time of King Herod, he sought to kill the apostles. He kills James with a sword and because he saw that it pleased the Jews, he captured Peter and threw him in prison intending to kill him. However, God had other plans. An angel came into the cell where Peter slept, woke him up and led him out of prison. And when Herod would have brought him forth, the same night Peter was sleeping between two soldiers, bound with two chains....And behold the angel of the Lord came to him and a light shined in the prison: and he smote Peter on the side, and raised him saying, "Arise up quickly" And his chains fell off from his hands "(Acts 12: 6-7).

As Peter followed the angel each door of the prison ward opened. When they came to the iron city gate of the city, it opened on its own accord! Until this time, Peter thought that he was in a vision having a good dream. When he came to himself he realized that he was free! This has to be the best prison break ever recorded in history.

Healing Angels – Angels are not only messengers of the Lord to bring encouragement and deliver God's people in the time of need, but they also minister healing. When Paul said, "Are they not all ministering spirits, sent forth to minister for them who shall be heirs of salvation, (He. 1:14) he includes the ministry of healing. Here is a Biblical example, there is at Jerusalem by the sheep market a pool, which is called in the Hebrew tongue Bethesda, having five porches. In these lay a great multitude of impotent folk, those that are blind, halt and withered, waiting for the moving of the water. For an angel went down in a certain season into the pool, and troubled the water: whosoever was the first one that stepped into the troubled water was made whole of whatsoever disease he had (John 5:2-4). It was not uncommon for the famous evangelist, William Branham to see angels ministering at his crusades. The Apostle of faith, Smith Wigglesworth, was also familiar with the ministry of angels that performed miraculous healings and deliverance at his crusades and meetings.

As word of wisdom, our dependence for ministry is not upon angels but the Lord Jesus Christ, for it is "by His stripes we are healed" (Is. 53:5). Ministering with angels is the joy of having our names written in heaven. This is exciting as we get to partake in the ministry that Jesus began on earth that continues through the body of Christ today.

Angels as Watchers – Angelic watchers know the times, seasons and cycles of the Lord. As timekeepers, they observe and monitor events that take place on the earth and the activities of

God's people and how they respond to fulfil their destiny.

As messengers, they often decree that which has been declared from the throne of God to men through a visitation, prophecy, vision or dream. We see this taking place when King Nebuchadnezzar, the King of Babylon, has a night vision, I saw in the vision of my head upon my bed, and behold, a watcher and a holy one came down from heaven (Daniel 4:13).

The Watcher in Nebuchadnezzar's dream is an angel. His assignment is to decree the words of the holy one – the Lord. Angels are authorized to convey the word of the Lord as noted in Nebuchadnezzar's vision when the angel proclaimed, "This matter is by the decree of the watchers, and the demand of the holy ones, to the intent that the living may know that the most High rules in the Kingdom of men ….(Da. 4:17)

Angels often give voice to the things of God. They have been given the authority to decree that which the Lord has commanded them to

Unravelling Psalm 91

speak. This is why the scripture often refers to the words that angels speak as the Word of the Lord, because of its source – the Lord Jesus Christ. Angels are authorized to speak on behalf of the Lord, which is why they are often referred to as "Angels of the Lord."

I believe that God is assigning Angelic Watchers to those that have the gift of prophetic vision with the ministry of intercession. As these Christians watch and wait upon the Lord, like the seers of the Old Testament, angels will come to them to offer insight, guidance and the wisdom of the Lord. These are the Sons of Issachar called to understand the times with the wisdom to properly prepare the people for the times, of the children of Issachar, there were men of understanding of the times, to know what Israel out to do" (1 Chronicles 12:32).

God wants to instruct the Church to ambush her enemies instead of being ambushed, avoid disaster and prevail in difficult times. It is the wisdom of God that Joseph counselled Pharaoh with the strategy that enabled Egypt to prosper during the seven years of drought that came upon Egypt. Such is the power of the gift of wisdom.

The gift of Wisdom is to know the mind of Christ in every situation. Although it is not as spectacular as the power gifts it is needful to make that which is known to become more effective and bear fruit. Prophetic revelation is simply knowledge that has no real guidance or direction. Wisdom imparts the counsel of Christ in regards to how to proceed with that which has been revealed that gives it purpose and direction.

Angels of Creativity – The first recorded act that God did was to create the heaven and the earth. (Ge. 1:1) As sons and daughters of the creator, there is natural creativity that is inherent in the DNA of mankind. I believe that angels on assignment are being released to impart creative ideas that will prosper the Church. One such area is that of creative finance. Instead of Church leadership looking to the congregation for its financial support, they will have God's wisdom to make creative investments in the marketplace.

The profits from this will enable the Church to provide for the poor, the oppressed and the widows, as well as to advance the Kingdom of God through missions. God is also empowering ministers of finance with the wisdom for creative investments to underwrite the armies of the living God. This will provide the financial support needed for those are strong in the Lord doing great exploits as a Kingdom Force to advance the gospel of the Kingdom.

As part of the creative release, we will see a tremendous anointing on the visual arts, such as paintings and sculpture. The anointing upon this artwork work will heal the sick and lead many to Christ. The ministry of creative writing by scribe angels will greatly impact the body of Christ. There is also a creative release to equip the body of Christ for the work of ministry through user-friendly technology.

The ministry of worship will come to a whole new level by the army of praise dancers and worshipping warriors that dance with angels. Worship leaders that dwell in heavenly places will release the sound of heaven accompanied by an angelic choir that will transform the lives of many. I once had an open vision of the Lord of Host's dwelling in His army. They were singing a new song as they marched forward, trampling upon the head of the enemy!

God has released ministering angels to assist the Church for the work of ministry that will ramp up the anointing to a whole new level. Every person has a guardian angel and every Church has an angel assigned to them (Rev.1:20). These are the angels of heaven called to work with the Church for "Thy Kingdom Come, your will be done, on earth as it is in heaven." You have at least one, and perhaps more! You too can operate at a higher level of anointing to impact

Unravelling Psalm 91

your sphere of influence with the full gospel of Jesus Christ that reveals the Kingdom of heaven on earth in power and demonstration.

Chapter 4
Debunk all fears

'Thou shalt tread upon the lion and adder: the young lion and the dragon shalt thou trample under feet. Because he hath set his love upon me, therefore will I deliver him: I will set him on high, because he hath known my name.'

The psalmist in psalm 62:11, 'God hath spoken once; twice have I heard this; that power belongeth unto God. Psalm 68:34-35; Isaiah 26:4; Mathew 6:13, Mathew 28:18; John 19:11; Revelation 19:1.

Ephesians 6:12 gives us an idea of the battle we are likely to face, and it is not a physical battle but a fierce contest against principalities, powers and rulers of the darkness of this world. Powers that are yet to be invented cannot have any effect on us rather they will remain under our feet. In chapter three is an indication that the angels, the **'heavenly forces'** are already on assignment with different roles just like you have in an organised paramilitary outfit and you can imagine how organised the Almighty can be and I wonder why many in Christendom nurse un-necessary fear.

2 Timothy 1:7, 'For God hath not given us the spirit of fear; but of power, and love, and a sound mind. Then let me ask you this simple question, why are you afraid? , Acts 20:24, Acts 21:13; Romans 8:15; Hebrew 2:15; 1Jn 4:18 , Micah 3:8; Zechariah 4:6; Luke10:19, Luke 24:49; Acts 1:8, Acts 6:8, Acts 9:22, Acts 10:38; 1Corintians 2:4. The issue here is that when you start to nurse fear before a battle, you are simply indicating that you have already conceded defeat before the battle is fought, we should have this scripture at the back of our mind, Jerimiah 32:27, 'Behold, I am the LORD, the God of all flesh: **is there anything too hard for me**?' and don't forget in a hurry Luke 1:37, 'For with God nothing shall be impossible.' , Luke 18:27; Genesis 18:14; Numbers 11:23; Job 13:2; Jerimiah 32:17, Zechariah 8:6; Mathew 19:26; Mark 10:27; Philippians 3:21.

What is that battle called? And our God can fix it. I shared this testimony in my book titled reaching high altitude with prayers, Let me share it once more to encourage us.

I had proceeded on vacation at my place of work and incidentally, we had a Job order which had to do with the deployment of an Automated Teller Machine at Bayero University branch at Kano, my colleague, Essien had to cover my bit and he was based at Kaduna which is under Northcentral. The machine had refused to come into service after installation had been concluded for 2 days and there was panic as the CEO spat fire and the message was clear that heads will roll. My Line manager at the Head office called me and instructed me to suspend my vacation and report to the site and look for how to resolve this issue.

Essien called and informed me that he had tried all the tactics and the machine refused to come into service and he is tired and wants to return to his base. I proceeded to the branch and my boss called after 3 minutes to inform me that he just got the information that I have just arrived at the site and I should ensure I get him posted with developments.

The scripture Jerimiah 32:27 was already in my heart and I remembered that the Lord in Ezekiel 37, dry and dead bones were transformed into a strong mighty army in the Land of Israel. What can't God do, even metals will obey the voice of the Lord.

I checked the Network Infrastructure it looked perfect, I had 5 minutes chat with the supplier of the Automated Teller Machine inquiring whether the machine was actually in order, He carried out a test in my presence that proved that the equipment was in order.

I informed the Project Manager that I will like to use the restroom, all eyes were on me and I was fully aware that in their hearts they will be saying, 'What Magic will Alex perform, Let us see', I prayed and told God that All power belongs to him and I had to stand upon his word in Jerimiah 32:27, I decreed that the metal should receive breath in the name of Jesus.

At the Automated machine room, I laid my hands on it and declared in the name of Jesus receive life and I instructed them to switch it on and my faith was very strong and after about 10 minutes the ATM came into service and the project manager jumped from his seat and proceeded to my direction and asked me a simple question, 'Alex what did you do?', while he was talking my boss at the head office called me and he said Alex what did you do and I told him, "The ancient of days helped me to solve the problem' and My boss said 'Be serious man, remember you are a technical person', the news was all over the head office.

Pain, anguish and anger were turned to Joy, this is what God can do, our Group Head would have lost his job and my boss was boasting at the head office saying, 'Alex is my man, I'm always confident when issues are handled by him', it is not true all the time I worked at this bank, I always depend on God the owner of Knowledge and wisdom to help me out and God has been faithful. Most times whenever I touch any ICT infrastructure it starts working and even when I send my staff they will ask him to call his boss, God was indeed faithful, You might say it's an electronic device and I will say Yes but God is the God of All flesh, contrary powers were subdued.

I want to remind us that we should not be afraid or nurse any fear because the Lord has taken care of all things and the enemy is under our feet.

Good Health

Bless the LORD, O my soul, And forget not all His benefits: Who forgives all your iniquities, Who heals all your diseases, Who redeems your life from destruction, Who crowns you with lovingkindness and tender mercies, Who satisfies your mouth with good things, So that your youth is renewed like the eagle's. The LORD executes righteousness And justice for all who are oppressed. (Psalms 103:2-6). Psalm 30:2, Psalm 38:1-7, Psalm 41:3-4, Psalm 41:8, Psalm 107:17-22, Psalm 147:3; Exodus15:26; Numbers 12:13, Numbers 21:7-9; Isaiah 33:24, Isaiah 53:5; Jerimiah 17:14; James 5:15.

The Bible rates health right near the top of the list in importance. A person's mind, spiritual nature, and body are all interrelated and interdependent. What affects one affects the others. If the body is misused, the mind and the spiritual nature cannot become what God planned they should be—and you won't be able to live an abundant life. (See John 10:10.)

God gave health principles because He knows what is best for the human body. Automobile manufacturers place an operation manual in the glove compartment of each new car because they know what is best for their creation. God, who made our bodies, also has an "operations manual." It is the Bible. Ignoring God's "operations manual" often results in disease, twisted thinking, and burned-out lives, just as abusing a car can result in serious car trouble. Following God's principles results in "saving health" (Psalm 67:2 KJV) and more abundant life (John 10:10). With our cooperation, God can use these great health laws to significantly reduce and eliminate the effects of the diseases of Satan (Psalm 103:2, 3).

A Christian will even eat and drink differently—all to the glory of God—choosing only "what is good." If God says a thing is not fit to eat, He must have a good reason. He is not a harsh dictator, but a loving Father. His counsel is for our good always. The Bible promises, "No good thing will He withhold from those who walk uprightly" (Psalm 84:11). So if God withholds a thing from us, it is because it is not good for us.

It is not impossible that we adhere to good living, eating the right and the enemy makes an attempt to inflict us with sickness and the Good news here is that Isaiah 53:5, 'But he was wounded for our transgressions, he was bruised for our iniquities: the chastisement of our peace was upon him, and with his stripes, we are healed.' But he was wounded for our transgressions, he was bruised for our iniquities, the chastisement of our peace was upon him and with his stripes, we are healed. (KJV)

But He was pierced through for our transgressions, He was crushed for our iniquities;

the punishment that brought us peace was on him, and by his wounds, we are healed. (NIV) And He bore our sins in His body on the cross, so that we might die to sin and live to righteousness; for by His wounds you were healed. 1 Peter 2:24 ESV

Both passages describe the physical punishment Christ took upon Himself for the sake of humanity—of those who chose to believe in Him. However, the passage in Isaiah is one of the most renowned Old Testament passages because it prophesied about Jesus 700 years before He arrived in a manger.

To understand the truth of these passages, let's look at both Isaiah 53:5 and 1st Peter 2:24 in context. But He was pierced through for our transgressions,

He was crushed for our iniquities; The chastening for our well-being fell upon Him And by His scourging, we are healed. Isaiah 53:5, and He bore our sins in His body on the cross, so that we might die to sin and live to righteousness; for by His wounds you were healed. 1 Peter 2:24

Unravelling Psalm 91

The first time we come across this passage is when Isaiah describes what about happen to Jesus. He describes the suffering of the Messiah and then writes the reasons for His suffering: He was pierced for our transgressions (rebellion) and crushed for our iniquities (depravity).

The prophet Isaiah was pointing out that our sins required an atonement. Our sins required forgiveness. Our sins need to be washed off each of us. But the traditional way God's people atoned for sin in the Old Testament was through the blood sacrifice of animals performed at the Temple. To provide atonement and to be washed of our sins, a perfect sacrifice was coming for all of mankind: God's only son, Jesus.

Whenever we address prophecy or prophets of the Bible, we need to understand individuals like Isaiah were sent by God to warn God's people, the Israelites. These warnings were often not heeded and largely ignored because they were called to repent of their sins and idolatries with the threat of punishment and sometimes reward.

It wasn't until many years later when scholars realized the words written by Isaiah and other prophets were fulfilled and true. Isaiah became a prophet of God around 742 BCE (found in Isaiah Chapter 6) when he describes seeing God for the first time. He then offered himself to God and was commissioned to give voice to the divine Word. When it comes to the subject of prophecy, 25 per cent of the Bible is a prophecy of how Jesus would be our Servant, King and Salvation.

It was commonly taught that the Messiah's role would be to restore the Kingdom of God but there was also a basis the He would suffer for His people too. However, the Jews at the time largely ignored Isaiah's warnings or predictions about the coming King despite the language in Isaiah 53 pointing to the suffering of an individual, not a nation like many assumed.

This passage in Isaiah is also known as the Hebrew poetic form called Parallelism. In Hebrew poetry, lines are repeated instead of rhyming which is found in English poetry. We find the first two lines are repeated to emphasize the idea that the Messiah would bleed for our sins. The second two lines repeated the concept of the punishments Jesus would talk upon Himself even though Jesus was blameless, perfect, pure and free from sin in every way. These last two lines also describe that His suffering would the cure and restoration for mankind.

The stripes mentioned by Isaiah were the awful lashings upon Jesus' back by the Roman whips. Thirty-nine stripes were the traditional punishment for a condemned prisoner. According to the scripture, these stripes upon Christ were on behalf of our healing (1 Peter 2:2). In 1st Peter 2:24, Peter also writes about the work of Jesus on the cross. He explains that Christ traded our sins for His life. He bore the punishment for our sins, the death we should have received instead of Him. Peter teaches that Jesus' actions were done so that we could live righteously and have salvation.

Just this week, I heard someone quote these scriptures in prayer as they prayed for the healing of a loved one. "Lord, Chris is in the hospital. We lift him to you, by your stripes he is healed." As the prayer ended, I wondered if it was my place to tell them, the scripture was taken out of context. The power of the cross wasn't meant for our physical healing, rather our spiritual healing.

These two passages are central to the topic of healing, however, they are misapplied and often misunderstood. The word "healed" when translated from both Greek and Hebrew can mean spiritual or physical healing. However the context of both Isaiah 53 and 1 Peter 2 make it clear that they are referring to spiritual healing, we are not unaware that the spiritual determines the physical. Have you realised that a sick person will seek medical attention and he is given a good bill of health, this fellow still feels sick? This implies that the spiritual must be resolved.

Immunity

holding fast to the Head, from whom all the body, nourished and knit together by joints and ligaments, grows with the increase that is from God. (Colossians 2:19)

Apostle Paul inspired by divine revelation advised the church to "hold fast to the head". The head that Paul was referring to, in the context of Colossians 2:19, is Christ. He was using the human anatomy to communicate spiritual truths. The same way the human brain rules the entire body, Christ rules the church.

God has uniquely designed our bodies with an immune system that can effectively tackle and resist any bacteria, germ or virus that may seek to interrupt our normal body function. The brain supervises the immune system of the body. And in like manner, Christ, the head of the church oversees the spiritual immune system of the body of Christ (the church). The natural immune system of our bodies is guaranteed to walk effectively. If it is not compromised or weakened by stress or the deliberate intake of harmful substances to the body

The good news is that the body of Christ has a better spiritual immune system that can never be compromised by any force or influence. Why? The omnipotent power of God is the immune system of the believer in Christ. That is the same "greatness of God's power" that is presently at work in all who believe in Christ (see Ephesians 1:19). It does change. As a child of God, you are not vulnerable. Your immune system is beyond the reach of any evil.

However, fear, anxiety, ignorance and unbelief can cause a temporal disconnect from the reality of the believer's spiritual immunity in Christ (see Ephesians 4:17). The devil knows this; hence, he constantly seeks to hijack what we believe about the truth with his lies. Sadly, once you believe the devil's lie, which is any information that is inconsistent with what the realities of your union with Christ, that lie immediately obscures the reality of your spiritual immunity in Christ. And also, creates doubts when you are faced with a challenge or crisis. Staying focused on the gospel maintains your spiritual immunity.

In the light of this, you must never give the devil and the reports of his manifestation any reverence. They are inferior facts compared to the facts of what is available to you in your union with Christ. He that dwells in you is greater than any demonic manifestation.

According to the Scriptures, God encircles, encompasses, covers and shields those who make Him their refuge. His presence—the anointing—is a kind of force field of protection making you inaccessible to the enemy no matter what the circumstances.

That's how men and women throughout the ages have been able to walk unharmed through all kinds of dangerous situations. That's how Daniel survived the lions' den. The lions couldn't get to him because a tangible force field of God's protection was around him (Daniel 6:16-22). God was Daniel's refuge in the lion pit.

And God was a refuge for Shadrach, Meshach and Abednego in the fiery furnace as well. They were faithful to God and believed God, and a circle of His power—the tangible force of God's anointing—encased them. They didn't bow and they didn't burn. They didn't even smell of smoke (Daniel 3:12-27). An angel "like the Son of God" was in the furnace with them. They were not alone, hallelujah! They were encompassed by the power of God!

That same protection belongs to us today when we dwell in the secret place of the Most High (Psalm 91:1). A thousand shall fall at thy side, and ten thousand at thy right hand; but it shall not come nigh thee. Only with thine eyes shalt thou behold and see the reward of the wicked. Because thou hast made the Lord, which is my refuge, even the most High, thy habitation;

there shall no evil befall thee, neither shall any plague come nigh thy dwelling. For he shall give his angels charge over thee, to keep thee in all thy ways (Psalm 91:7-11).

The Spirit of God told me this concerning the secret place: There is a place in Christ Jesus where we abide in the secret place of God's protection. The world knows nothing about this secret place, nor can they live there. It is a place revealed by the Holy Spirit. It is for the obedient. Our lives are hidden with Christ in God. (See Colossians 3:3.) You and I can live in a secret place. Wherever we go, that secret place goes with us, surrounding and encircling us.

Chapter Five

Dominion Unleashed

There are about 400 billion stars in our galaxy alone. It is amazing when you think about it. The Milky Way isn't even very big. Every star has an approximate average of 1.6 planets. So, if you do the arithmetic, that's 650 billion planets. The Earth is home to roughly 2 billion species of life. Some 70 to 90% of those species are bacteria. There might be a total of 40 million insect species. Yet, our science is just in its infancy. Some 10,000 species are discovered each year. To date, only about 1.5 million species have been described, and less than 1% of those are bacteria. Of those two billion species (or 1.5 million species we have named), almost 60 thousand are vertebrates, 5 thousand are mammals, and 350 are primates. Human beings are but one of them.

While the universe has been around for 13.772 billion years, we homo sapiens have only been around some 300,000 years. If my middle school math days serve me well, 13.772 billion minus 300,000 is still 13.772 billion — in other words, we've not been around long enough for our history to be within the order of significant digits.

Despite evidence to the contrary, many of us have been taught to think of our place in the world with an outrageous and unjust logic — the universe is ours and it exists for the taking.

But this logic doesn't just stop with anthropocentrism. Let's follow this logic down a little further. Of the 7.6 billion human beings on the planet, how many have access to clean drinking water, a healthy diet, good health care, a quality education, a living wage, etc? A little more than half of them are men. Of those 3.8 billion men, how many of us are white, cis-gendered, heterosexual, Christian, American? All of these characteristics are things that I share with most of our national leaders, almost all of our nation's past presidents, and the richest man on the face of the earth. I find it curious and scary to believe that such a small portion of the world's population has believed for so long that the world was made for them. But let us not be naïve, most of us humans think the same way about our relationship to the rest of Creation. Domination, see, comes in many forms.

This unjust logic of ours, our model of society, our understanding of the meaning of life, the way human beings have perceived themselves concerning the rest of Creation — at least for the last four hundred years or so — has almost entirely shaped our way of life. It is hard to disagree with liberation theologian, Leonardo Boff, when he described the modern human. Most of us live, he said, as if the most important thing in life is to accumulate vast amounts of the means of life — material wealth, goods, and services — to enjoy our short journey on this planet. In achieving this purpose we are aided by science, which comprehends how the Earth functions, and technology, which acts upon it for human benefit. And this is to be done as speedily as possible. Hence, we strive for maximum profit with a minimum investment in the shortest possible time. In this type of cultural practice, human beings are regarded as above things, making use of them for their enjoyment, never as alongside things, members of a larger planetary and cosmic community. The ultimate result, which is only now becoming strikingly visible, is contained in an expression attributed to Gandhi: The Earth is enough for everyone's needs but not for everyone's greed.

In other words, our basic model for relating to each other — how we know what life is all about — is domination. When we see ourselves as being above rather than alongside, we operate within a framework — a logic — of domination.

I want to draw your attention to a specific biblical landmine. This is one of the most referenced passages when it comes to Creation, justice, and the role of Christianity in the world: Genesis 1. It's not so much an entire passage or even a verse it's just one word: dominion.

Unravelling Psalm 91

This entire chapter is a beautiful and poetic description of God's relationship with Creation. That's why it's so unfortunate that when it is read with the intent of asking what our relationship to Creation should be, Christians tend to narrow in on this one word. And this is specifically true when you talk about the relationship between human beings and other non-human animals. God said, "Let us make humankind in our image, according to Our likeness; and let them have dominion..."

Dominion? "Didn't God set human beings over Creation? Didn't God give people dominion over animals and doesn't that mean we can... [kill them, eat them, wear them, cage them, experiment with them, fill in the blank]?"

First off, the word dominion is repeated twice. That must mean it was important to the scribe or scribes that used it. But that should never, ever, trump what God said about Creation at every step along the way, "It is good." For God to declare these things to be good, especially animal life, even before human beings existed, implies that they are valuable in their own right — that God delights in them. As a Jewish scholar, Roberta Kalechofsky points out, "this substantiates the view that animals were regarded as integral subjects. God's [expressed] delight in these creations…does not reflect a god who created animal life to be in bondage."

(Roberta Kalechofsky, "Hierarchy, Kinship, and Responsibility: The Jewish Relationship to the Animal World," in A Communion of Subjects: Animals in Religion, Science, and Ethics, edited by Paul Waldau and Kimberly Patton (New York: Columbia University Press, 2006)

Dominion is mentioned twice in verse 28, in the very following verse (Genesis 1:29), God says, "See, I have given you every plant yielding seed that is upon the face of all the earth, and every tree with seed in its fruit; you shall have them for food." In other words, whatever dominion humans have been granted over animals, it doesn't involve eating them. Even more, if we're going to be using this passage to understand our relationship with Creation, we must be constrained first and foremost by our reverence for the fact that God took delight in what God created. God said, "It is good."

It has been said that if kings and queens exercised dominion over their subjects the way human beings do over the other animals, kings and queens would have no subjects. So why is being in God's image often interpreted given power, manipulation, and hegemony instead of compassion, mercy, and emptying unconditional love? We often anthropomorphize God as powerful, fierce, and angry (if not belligerent). When we are lording over others, using power — it is then that we are most likely to assert the image of God. Acts of unconditional love, suspensions of judgment, mercy for the weak, and kindness to animals get associated with a wishy-washy picture of who Jesus was but are rarely discussed regarding God the Creator.

(Carol J. Adams, "What About Dominion in Genesis?" p. 2. , 1997)

We need to understand that God created man in his image and likeness, I agree that man was given dominion over creation and the fact remains that someone must be put in charge. In the context of this book, God sent his son to the world to liberate mankind from sin and Isaiah 22:22 indicated that 'And the key of the house of David will I lay upon his shoulder; so he shall open, and none shall shut, and he shall shut, and none shall open.' They have been laid upon his shoulder means dominion over principalities, power and rulers of darkness. Mathew 16:18-19; Revelation 1:18, Keys of heaven, hell and death was handed to Jesus interestingly after the resurrection.

We need to understand that these keys automatically fall upon our shoulders (Romans 8:17) and this means because of our inheritance the dominion falls upon us and we can equally make decrees and declarations and it will come to pass. There is power in the tongue when we make confessions and it will come to pass and this attribute for reasons, we need to adhere to a composite prerequisite, confession of any magnitude comes to pass. I deliberately quoted carol on his explanation of dominion which cantered on creation but in our context, we are looking at dominion concerning warfare and we cannot afford to be gentle rather we take the bull by the horn and take authority.

When we recite psalm 91 we make confessions that remind us of our relationship with God and most importantly clinging to the promises that are accrued to us as his heir and most times all we need is to exercise faith concerning this psalm and we earn our desired victory.

What is in the curse of the law that Christ has redeemed us from? Sin, sickness, pain, suffering, and death- are all part of the curse of the law- and we have been redeemed from it all!

Deuteronomy 28:15-25 "However, if you do not obey the Lord your God and do not carefully follow all his commands and decrees I am giving you today, all these curses will come on you and overtake you: You will be cursed in the city and cursed in the country. Your basket and your kneading trough will be cursed. The fruit of your womb will be cursed, and the crops of your land, and the calves of your herds and the lambs of your flocks. You will be cursed when you come in and cursed when you go out.

The Lord will send on you curses, confusion and rebuke in everything you put your hand to until you are destroyed and come to sudden ruin because of the evil you have done in forsaking him. The Lord will plague you with diseases until he has destroyed you from the land you are entering to possess. The Lord will strike you with wasting disease, with fever and inflammation, with scorching heat and drought, with blight and mildew, which will plague you until you perish. The sky over your head will be bronze, the ground beneath you iron. The Lord will turn the rain of your country into dust and powder; it will come down from the skies until you are destroyed. The Lord will cause you to be defeated before your enemies. You will come at them from one direction but flee from them in seven, and you will become a thing of horror to all the kingdoms on earth."

Sickness and disease are listed as a curse of the law in the Bible. But Christ HAS redeemed us from the curse of the law!! Christ bore the curse of the law on the cross. He has redeemed us NOT just for sin- but also from all sickness and disease.

Unravelling Psalm 91

Chapter 6
Longevity Assured

'I will set him on high because he hath known my name. He shall call upon me, and I will answer him: I will be with him in trouble; I will deliver him and honour him. With long life will I satisfy him and show him my salvation.'

I will set him on high because he hath known my name, because you have known his name means that there exists a cordial relationship with God. Doing his will and living a holy life this is not negotiable, this makes you the apple of God's eye(Zechariah 2:8), 'For this is what the LORD of Hosts says: "After His glory has sent me against the nations that have plundered you-for whoever touches you touches the apple of His eye'. When you become the apple of God's eye what are the implications?

The apple of one's eye is a very sensitive place and therefore very protected. Think about your eye for a moment. What happens if something flies in it or toward it? Your eyelids reflexively close, your head turns, and your hands position themselves to ward off the threat. Our eyesight is valuable, and our body naturally protects that vulnerable spot to prevent injury.

So, the instruction in Proverbs 7:2 is to hold godly wisdom in high regard as the valuable thing it is. The prayer in Psalm 17:8 is for God to keep guard over us as He would the pupil of His eye. And the description of God's care for His people in Deuteronomy 32:10 emphasizes Israel's vulnerability and God's tender, loving affection. God provided complete protection; His people were a priority. In the "howling wilderness," God provided manna for them to eat, water from a rock, and safety from their enemies. His care was as automatic as if He were guarding the centre of His eye from harm. What a loving God we serve.

God held the Israelites as the apple of His eye, rebellious and stiff-necked though they were in the wilderness. Being the apple of His eye, they were most cherished. And God's care for His people has not diminished with time. He holds His children close, and He can protect us as easily as our eyelids protect our pupils. He does this because He loves us in Christ. He has a parental, protective love for us, and the biblical descriptions of His love are eye-opening, to say the least.

Even when the Lamb of God had been sent to this world, Philippians 2:10-11 tells us at the mention of the name of Jesus, 'That at the name of Jesus every knee should bow, of things in heaven, and **things in earth**, and **things under the earth**; And that every tongue should confess that Jesus Christ is Lord, to the glory of God the Father.' There is enormous power in this name that 'things in earth' and 'things under the earth' would bow to that name, it is a great privilege to be associated to this name and this is the reason why the name is not only mentioned but screamed when in a midst of a challenge. Knowing this name makes a huge difference.

He shall call upon me, and I will answer him: I will be with him in trouble; This statement requires a serious commitment from our end as children of

God, Acts 10:34, peter asserted that God is a respecter of no person but principles before this statements can be honoured, is not far from when we carry out transactions at a bank branch, our accounts must be funded, signature confirmed to be regular before the transaction can take place. This is the same, apart from remaining on track we must adhere to the principles, Psalm 50:14-15 says, 'Offer unto God **thanksgiving**; and **pay thy vows** unto the most High: And call upon me in the day of trouble: I will deliver thee, and thou shalt glorify me.' Other principles that are not mentioned
like **tithing, sacrificial giving, witnessing** – bearing fruit and the fruit abide, these are principles that will make us a cordial relationship with God. Once the principles are fulfilled, then the promise made will be fulfilled.

I will deliver him and honour him. With long life will I satisfy him and show him my salvation, "length of days;" that is, days lengthened out or multiplied. The meaning is, I will give him length of days as he desires, or until he is satisfied with life; implying that it is natural to desire long life; that long life is to be regarded as a blessing (compare Proverbs 3:2, Proverbs 3:16; Exodus 20:12); that religion tends to lengthen out life; since virtue, temperance, regular industry, the calmness of mind, moderation in all things, freedom from excesses in eating and in drinking - to all of which religion prompts - contribute to health, and length of days (see Psalm 34:12-14, notes; Psalm 37:9, note; Psalm 55:23, note).

And that a time will come, even under this promised blessing of the length of days, when a man will be "satisfied" with living; when he will have no strong desire to live longer; when, under the infirmities of advanced years, and under his lonely feelings from the fact that his early friends have fallen, and under the influence of a bright hope of heaven, he will feel that he has had enough of life here and that it is better to depart to another world.

Shew him my salvation - In another life, after he shall be "satisfied" with this life. The promise extends beyond the grave: "Godliness is profitable unto all things, having promise of the life that now is, and of that which is to come." See the notes at 1 Timothy 4:8. Thus, religion blesses man in this life and blesses him forever. In possession of this, it is a great thing to him to live long; and then it is a great thing to die - to go to be forever with God.

For us, to key into any scripture, we must live a holy life and ensure we maintain and keep to the principles this is not negotiable.

www.ingramcontent.com/pod-product-compliance
Lightning Source LLC
Chambersburg PA
CBHW051657040426
42446CB00009B/1180